A Garbage Truck's Day

T0014987

by Rebecca Sabelko
Illustrated by Christos Skaltsas

BLASTOFF!
MISSIONS

BELLWETHER MEDIA
MINNEAPOLIS, MN

BLASTOFF! MISSIONS

Blastoff! Missions takes you on a learning adventure! Colorful illustrations and exciting narratives highlight cool facts about our world and beyond. Read the mission goals and follow the narrative to gain knowledge, build reading skills, and have fun!

Traditional Nonfiction

BLASTOFF! READERS

BLASTOFF! Beginners

BLASTOFF! DISCOVERY

BLASTOFF! MISSIONS

Narrative Nonfiction

Blastoff! Universe

MISSION GOALS

> FIND YOUR SIGHT WORDS IN THE BOOK.

> LEARN ABOUT DIFFERENT KINDS OF GARBAGE TRUCKS.

> LEARN ABOUT THE DIFFERENT PARTS OF GARBAGE TRUCKS.

This edition first published in 2024 by Bellwether Media, Inc.

No part of this publication may be reproduced in whole or in part without written permission of the publisher. For information regarding permission, write to Bellwether Media, Inc., Attention: Permissions Department, 6012 Blue Circle Drive, Minnetonka, MN 55343.

Library of Congress Cataloging-in-Publication Data

Names: Sabelko, Rebecca, author.
Title: A garbage truck's day / by Rebecca Sabelko.
Other titles: Blastoff! missions. Machines at work.
Description: Minneapolis, MN : Bellwether Media, Inc., 2024. | Series: Blastoff! Missions: Machines at work | Includes bibliographical references and index. | Audience: Ages 5-8 | Audience: Grades 2-3 | Summary: "Vibrant illustrations accompany information about the daily activities of a garbage truck. The narrative nonfiction text is intended for students in kindergarten through third grade." -- Provided by publisher.
Identifiers: LCCN 2023014286 (print) | LCCN 2023014287 (ebook) | ISBN 9798886873863 (library binding) | ISBN 9798886875249 (paperback) | ISBN 9798886875744 (ebook)
Subjects: LCSH: Refuse collection vehicles--Juvenile literature. | Refuse collection--Juvenile literature. | Refuse collectors-Juvenile literature. | CYAC: Refuse collection vehicles. | Refuse collection. | Refuse collectors. | LCGFT: Instructional and educational works.
Classification: LCC TD794 .S23 2024 (print) | LCC TD794 (ebook) | DDC 628.4/42--dc23/eng/20230403
LC record available at https://lccn.loc.gov/2023014286
LC ebook record available at https://lccn.loc.gov/2023014287

Text copyright © 2024 by Bellwether Media, Inc. BLASTOFF! MISSIONS and associated logos are trademarks and/or registered trademarks of Bellwether Media, Inc.

Editor: Christina Leaf   Designer: Andrea Schneider

Printed in the United States of America, North Mankato, MN.

This is **Blastoff Jimmy**! He is here to help you on your mission and share fun facts along the way!

Table of Contents

Morning in the Yard

yard

It is early morning.
The garbage truck waits
with others in the **yard**.

The collectors arrive and get
their **routes**. They are ready to
drive their trucks around town!

collectors

These collectors get their truck ready.
The driver starts the truck.
The other collector makes sure
everything works safely.
Time to start the route!

front
loader

Different kinds of trucks drive out of the yard first.

A **side loader** goes to neighborhoods filled with homes. That **front loader** goes to work sites.

side loader

9

The **rear loader** heads to homes and businesses. It turns onto a quiet street. Bins sit outside of each house.

It is time to pick up the garbage!

bins

rear loader

The truck pulls up to its first stop. The collector puts the bin on the truck's lift.

She uses a **lever** on the truck to empty the bin into the **hopper**.

JIMMY SAYS ► There are some things garbage trucks cannot pick up. People must find safe ways to get rid of paint, some light bulbs, televisions, and many other items.

lift

hopper

Next, she pulls the **packer blade** lever. The blade squashes the garbage inside the container. Now there is more room!

packer blade

lever

container

The collector hops onto the back of the truck. They will do the whole street!

Later, the truck must stop at some businesses. The collector rolls a small **dumpster** to the truck.

By early afternoon, the truck finishes the route. It made hundreds of stops!

dumpster

The truck is packed with garbage! It goes to the **landfill**.

The back of the truck lifts. A **panel** pushes the garbage out and into the landfill.

landfill

The empty truck goes back to the yard. The collectors clean the truck.

It is ready to pick up more garbage tomorrow!

Garbage Truck Jobs

load garbage

squash garbage

take garbage to the landfill

Glossary

dumpster–a large container that holds garbage

front loader–a type of garbage truck that lifts dumpsters from the front of the truck

hopper–the part of a garbage truck where garbage is emptied before it is squashed inside the container

landfill–a place where garbage trucks empty the garbage they collect

lever–a bar used to control a part of a garbage truck

packer blade–a large blade that squashes garbage inside the container to create more room

panel–a large plate that pushes garbage out of a garbage truck's container and into a landfill

rear loader–a type of garbage truck in which garbage is placed in the back of the truck

routes–assigned paths garbage trucks drive to pick up garbage

side loader–a type of garbage truck that lifts garbage bins from the side of the truck

yard–the place where garbage trucks are kept when they are not being used

To Learn More

AT THE LIBRARY

Alan, Jon. *Let's Talk About Garbage Trucks.* Minneapolis, Minn.: Gray Duck Creative Works, 2021.

Leaf, Christina. *Garbage Collectors.* Minneapolis, Minn.: Bellwether Media, 2019.

Sterling, Charlie W. *Where Does Garbage Go?* Minneapolis, Minn.: Jump!, 2021.

ON THE WEB

FACTSURFER

Factsurfer.com gives you a safe, fun way to find more information.

1. Go to www.factsurfer.com.

2. Enter "garbage trucks" into the search box and click 🔍.

3. Select your book cover to see a list of related content.

BEYOND THE MISSION

> WHAT PART OF THE GARBAGE TRUCK'S DAY DID YOU THINK WAS THE MOST INTERESTING?

> WOULD YOU LIKE TO DRIVE A GARBAGE TRUCK? WHY OR WHY NOT?

> THINK UP A NEW LEVER FOR A GARBAGE TRUCK. WHAT DOES IT DO? HOW DOES IT WORK?

Index